Phonics At Home

Kate Robinson

BLOOMSBURY EDUCATION
Bloomsbury Publishing Plc
50 Bedford Square, London, WC1B 3DP, UK
BLOOMSBURY, BLOOMSBURY EDUCATION and the Diana logo are trademarks of Bloomsbury Publishing Plc
First published in Great Britain, 2020 by Bloomsbury Publishing Plc

Bloomsbury Publishing Plc does not have any control over, or responsibility for, any third-party websites referred to or in this book. All internet addresses given in this book were correct at the time of going to press. The author and publisher regret any inconvenience caused if addresses have changed or sites have ceased to exist, but can accept no responsibility for any such changes

A catalogue record for this book is available from the British Library

ISBN: PB: 978-1-4729-5515-9; ePDF: 978-1-4729-5514-2; ePub: 978-1-4729-5516-6

2 4 6 8 10 9 7 5 3 1

Text design by Sarah Malley

Printed and bound by CPI Group (UK) Ltd, Croydon, CR0 4YY

All papers used by Bloomsbury Publishing Plc are natural, recyclable products from wood grown in well managed forests. The manufacturing processes conform to the environmental regulations of the country of origin

To find out more about our authors and books visit www.bloomsbury.com and sign up for our newsletters

Contents

Introduction   6

How to use this book   7

What is phonics and how does it work?   **8-11**
Phonics for reading   9
Phonics for spelling   10
What are phonemes and graphemes?   11

How children are taught phonics   **12-21**
1. Hearing individual sounds   12
2. Hearing sounds in spoken words   12
3. Splitting spoken words into sounds   14
    and blending sounds into spoken words
4. Matching sounds and letters   15
5. Reading or spelling words   19
How words are built – vowels and consonants   20
Order in which words are introduced   21

Tricky words and non-phonics-based methods   **23**

GAMES   **26-85**

How to choose and use the games   **27**

Games for hearing sounds   **29-33**
What's in the box?   29
Our kitchen band   30
Mirror my sound song   31
Story sound effects   32
The whisper chain   33

Games for hearing sounds in words   **34-39**
Find me a match   34
Where's the pair?   35
Sneaky sound sets   36
My sounds scrapbook   37
Fun phonics shopping   38
Same sound Sonja and Simon   39

Games for splitting words into sounds   **40-46**
and blending sounds into words
Sounds into words; words into sounds   40
Word chain   42
Sing the sounds   43
Island hopping   44
The big, bold action blend   45

Games for matching sounds and letters   **47-59**
Match the letter   47
Perfect pairs   48
Lovely large letters   49
Making graphemes   50
Terribly tickly letters   51
Letters of the week   52
Write the letter   53
Hidden letters   54
The grapheme twist   56
The grapheme monster chase   58
The grapheme stepping stones   59

Games for reading and spelling words   **60-79**

Plate of words   60
The skittle alley word build   62
Word match   64
Lots of lovely ladder words   66
Lollipop stick word build   68
Build words on pictures   70
Grapheme stick man   72
Twisting towers   74
Sentence spies   76
Cut and swap   78
Sentence builder   79

Further games for tricky or difficult words   **80-86**

Feel and read   80
Lovely large words   82
Feel and write   83
Wordplay   84
Get the meaning, fill the gap   85
Look, say, trace, cover, write   86

Sound List   88
Word List   90
List of Suffixes   94
Glossary   95
References   96

Introduction

Hello and well done!
You want to help your child with phonics, you've got the book and you've made it to the first chapter: you're on track!

Now, you're probably keen to know whether this book will answer some **key questions**.

What is **phonics** and how does it work?

The word **phonics** is used a lot in schools and books and on websites about reading and spelling. But what does the word actually mean? In this book you'll find clear and straightforward explanations of what phonics is, how phonics works and how children are taught phonics.

How can I help with phonics at home and can I make it **fun?**

You'll find lots of games and activities that will help children to develop their pre-reading, reading and spelling skills using phonics. All the games are fun and easy to play at home.

Why is phonics so important?

Phonics is the main approach used in schools for helping children to read words. It is also a key approach in teaching children how to spell.

There's lots of evidence that phonics is the best approach for almost every child, giving them a really good understanding of how sounds and letters build words. In 2006, the UK government carried out a review of all of the research into how children are taught to read and spell. This review, known as the Rose Review, found that most children learn to read and spell words best if phonics is the main method used for teaching and learning (Rose, 2006).

So, helping with phonics at home can make **a big difference** to your child's confidence and progress with reading and writing. And that can make a big difference to their confidence and progress in all areas of their life.

How to use this book

For an **introduction to phonics** and **how it works**, start at the next section: 'What is phonics and how does it work?'.

If you have a general understanding of phonics, but want **to grasp it in more depth**, turn to the section 'How children are taught phonics' on page 12.

For help **selecting the right games** and activities for your child, or **choosing the right letters or words** to focus on, turn to the section 'How to choose and use the games' on page 27.

If you just want to **browse through the games**, choose from the different sections of games on the **Contents** page and then look for a game that's right for your child.

Once you have chosen a game to play, think about **when and how to introduce it to your child**. Try to keep it fun and relaxed: choose a time when your child is not tired, hungry or grumpy. Go for short, regular bursts, such as ten minutes a day, a few days a week, rather than long stretches. It's better to stop when your child still wants to play more – that way they will be extra keen next time you play!

abcdefghijklm
nopqrstuvwxyz
abcdefghijklm
nopqrstuvwxyz
abcdefghijklm

**What is phonics
and how does it work?**

nopqrstuvwxyz
abcdefghijklm
nopqrstuvwxyz
abcdefghijklm
nopqrstuvwxyz

We build spoken words by **blending** together individual sounds. We write words by using individual letters, or small groups of letters, to represent each sound.

sh   i   p

Phonics is a method of learning to read and spell that focuses on these individual sounds and the letters that represent them.

Phonics for reading

When reading an unfamiliar word, children see the individual letters, or groups of letters, in the word, and remember the sounds that they each represent.

So, if your child wants to read the word **ship**, they first need to identify the familiar letters or letter groups in the word one by one: **sh**, then **i**, then **p**.

As they do this, they need to remember the sounds that each of those letters, or letter groups, represent. Finally, they can blend the sounds together and listen to the word that the sounds make: '**sh**' '**i**' '**p**': '**ship**'.

9

Phonics for spelling

When spelling an unfamiliar word, children hear the individual sounds in the spoken word and remember the letters, or groups of letters, that represent those sounds.

So, if your child wants to write the word **ship**, they first need to split the spoken word '**ship**' into all the different sounds that it contains: '**sh**' '**i**' and '**p**'.

They then need to remember which letters, or letter groups, are used to represent those sounds: sh, i and p, and then write those letters down in order.

What are phonemes and graphemes?

Understanding some key words

To understand phonics, it helps to understand a few key words.
The most important of these are the words **phoneme** and grapheme:

A **phoneme** is a single sound.

The sound '**sh**' is one phoneme.

The spoken word '**ship**' has three phonemes: '**sh**' '**i**' and '**p**'.

A grapheme is a letter, or group of letters, that represents one sound.
Each sound, or **phoneme**, is represented in writing by a grapheme –
a letter or group of letters.

The written word 'ship' has three graphemes: sh, i and p.

There are a few other specialist words that you will come across in this book. These are explained in the text and in reminder panels:

TERMINOLOGY

Blending sounds:
*joining sounds together to build whole words, e.g. '*c – a – t*' becomes '*cat*'*

There is also a glossary on page 95, where specialist words and phrases are listed and explained.

How children are taught phonics

Children's understanding and use of phonics is developed in steps.

Steps for developing phonics skills

1. Hearing individual sounds

2. Hearing individual sounds in words

3. Splitting spoken words into sounds and blending sounds into spoken words

Then, cycles of:

4. Matching sounds and letters

5. Reading or spelling words

Alongside this, children are also shown:

Additional non-phonic methods for reading and spelling tricky words

1. Hearing individual sounds

To read and spell words, your child needs to be able to match letters to sounds and sounds to letters.

To do this, they first need to get good at hearing individual sounds – picking out one sound from a group of sounds, matching sounds that are the same, and hearing and remembering all the different sounds in a string of sounds. You can help them with this by playing sound games. You'll find lots of games for helping your child hear sounds on pages 29-39.

2. Hearing sounds in spoken words

When your child has learnt to hear, match and copy individual sounds, they can practise identifying individual sounds within words. So, for example, they can match objects that start with the same sound.

You'll find lots of games for helping your child identify sounds within words on pages 40-46.

How to pronounce sounds

We often add an extra 'er' sound when pronouncing individual sounds. This can confuse children.

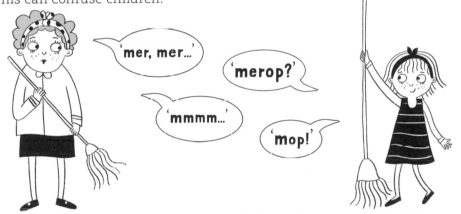

Watch out for that extra 'er' on the end of sounds and try to avoid it. As a guide, the chart below gives some letters and the right and wrong ways to pronounce the sounds they represent. For extra help, there are also lots of videos online showing how to clearly pronounce all of the sounds.

Letter	Incorrect pronunciation	Correct pronunciation
m	mer/me	mmmm
s	ser/se	sssss
l	ler/le	lllll
r	rer/re	rrrr
p	per/pe	p

3. Splitting spoken words into sounds and blending sounds into spoken words

Splitting

Once your child can identify an individual sound in a spoken word, they can move on to splitting spoken words into all of their individual sounds. This is also known as **segmenting**.

Your child will use segmenting for spelling: they'll split spoken words into separate sounds. Then they'll remember which letters represent each of those sounds.

Blending

Your child can also practise hearing individual sounds and joining them together to find a whole word. This is called **blending**.

Your child will use blending when reading. They remember the different sounds that each letter or letter group in a written word makes, then **blend** those sounds together to find a spoken word.

How to identify individual sounds

Sometimes it's hard to tell whether we're hearing one or more sounds. Take '**straight**' for example:

str aigh t

three sounds   one sound   one sound

Basically, if your lips, teeth, tongue or throat make more than one movement whilst making a sound, then you are making more than one distinct sound or phoneme. The Sound List at the back of the book shows you the 44 different sounds that we use in English. Likewise, the Word Lists show you over 100 different ways that we have for spelling those sounds.

4. Matching sounds and letters

As your child learns to identify separate sounds within spoken words, you can start to introduce the letters, or **graphemes**, that represent those sounds.

Order for introducing new letters

Schools and phonics programmes generally introduce all the **graphemes** in the same order.

They start with the graphemes that are easiest to build simple words with. Below is a list of the first graphemes introduced. For a full list, see the Word Lists at the back of the book.

s	sat, sap, sit, Sam, gas
a	an, at, Sam, sat
t	at, sat, tin, top, tap
p	pat, sap, pot
i	pin, bit, pip, dip, it, is
n	pin, an, in, nip, tin, nap, tan
m	mat, man, map, Sam, am, Mam
d	Dad, sad, did, Sid, dip, din
g	got, gap, tag, pig, gas
o	top, not, got, dog, God, pot
c	cat, cup, cot, cop, cod
k	kit, kid, Kim, Ken
ck	sock, sack, kick
e	get, pet, ten
u	up, mum, run, mug, sun, tuck
r	rim, rip, rat, rug, rocket
h	had, him, his, hut, hop, hug, has, hat
b	big, but, bad, Ben, bat, bed, bug, bag, bus
f	if, fit, fig, fun, fog
ff	puff, cuff, huff, off
l	lap, lot, let, leg, lit
ll	doll, Nell, dull, Bill, fill, bell, tell, sell
ss	less, hiss, pass, kiss, Tess, fuss, mess

How to pace introducing new graphemes

Introduce new graphemes for reading or spelling slowly, giving your child time to get used to new ones before adding more. Remember too that reading is easier than spelling. There are many words that your child will be able to read a long time before they are ready to learn to spell them.

Matching sounds and letters – tricky bits

When introducing new letters and sounds, there are a few issues you need to bear in mind.

TOP TIP:
Saying **out loud** some of the highlighted words below will help you to hear the similarities and differences more clearly.

Some letters can represent more than one different sound.

Think about the letter **C**.

It can represent the first sound in '**cat**'. It can also represent the first sound in '**celery**'.

Some sounds can be represented by various different letters or letter groups.

Think about the sound in the middle of '**feet**'.

> It can be represented by a double **ee**, e.g. f**ee**t, k**ee**p
> It can be represented by an **ea**, e.g. t**ea**cher, r**ea**d, n**ea**t
> It can be represented by a **y**, e.g. happ**y**, worr**y**, sill**y**
> It can be represented by **e_e**, e.g. th**eme**, d**ele**te

Some letter groups are strange! For example:

Quiet r
The three graphemes **er**, **ure** and **ur** can all represent the same sound and all contain the letter r. Yet, most accents do not pronounce the **r**:
teach**er** bak**er**   furnit**ure** creat**ure**   f**ur** t**ur**n c**ur**tain

Silent letters
There are graphemes with 'silent' letters – letters that do not affect the sound being represented at all:
knife **kn**ot   thu**mb** la**mb**   ba**tch** hu**tch**

Multi-letter graphemes
Some single sounds are represented by large groups of letters:
h**igh** r**igh**t **eigh**t n**eigh** stra**igh**t br**ough**t f**ough**t ca**ugh**t d**augh**ter

Odd sounds
Some graphemes, like **ng**, represent odd sounds:
ri**ng**   ba**ng**   ru**ng**   so**ng**   le**ng**th

However, most words in English do fit into a pattern
Most words can be placed into groups in which the same sounds are represented by the same letters.

c	c	ee	ea	y	e_e	ea
cat	city	feet	teacher	happy	these	head
comb	celery	keep	read	worry	discrete	bread
cub	ice	steel	neat	busy	theme	lead (the metal)
cold	space	freeze	please	silly	delete	read (past tense)
class	pencil	knee	sea	funny	extreme	

17

Highlight the patterns!

Patterns help your child to learn, remember and build their knowledge. So, when using whole words to introduce letters and sounds to your child, use groups of words that have the same letter, or letters, representing the same sound. Here's an example using the sounds in the word 'sea':

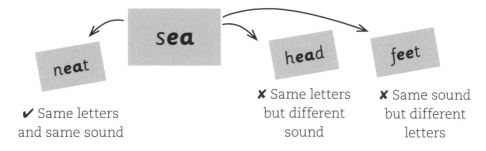

neat

✔ Same letters and same sound

sea

head

✘ Same letters but different sound

feet

✘ Same sound but different letters

Words in which the same sound is made by different letters, or in which the same letters make a different sound, are best taught in their own groups at a different time. In this way, children get to know the patterns and are not confused.

You'll find lots of games for introducing letters and sounds on pages 26-85. The Word Lists at the back of the book provide sets of words that follow the same pattern to use in games and activities.

TERMINOLOGY

Grapheme:
a letter or group of letters that represents one sound, e.g. sh, t or ck

TOP TIP:
The match between a sound and the letter, or group of letters, that represents that sound is called 'phoneme–grapheme correspondence'. So, two or more words that have the same sound represented by the same letter, or letters, are called 'words with the same phoneme–grapheme correspondence'. A good example is **ee**, e.g. freeze, keep, knee, feet.

5. Reading and spelling words

Reading whole words

When your child can match a few sounds and letters, you can introduce written words, helping your child to identify each letter or letter group (**grapheme**), to remember the sound that each **grapheme** represents and then to blend those sounds together to make a word.

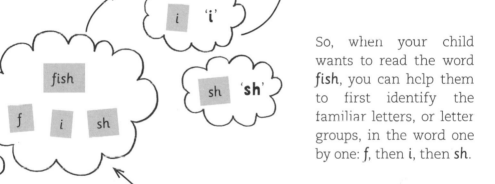

So, when your child wants to read the word *fish*, you can help them to first identify the familiar letters, or letter groups, in the word one by one: *f*, then *i*, then **sh**.

As they do this, you can help them to remember the sounds that each of those letters, or letter groups, represent.

Finally, you can help them to string the sounds together and listen to the word that they make: '**f**', '**i**' and '**sh**' makes '**fish**'.

19

Spelling whole words

You can also introduce whole spoken words for your child to spell, helping them to hear the individual sounds in the spoken word and to remember and write the letters, or groups of letters, that represent those sounds:

For example, if your child wants to write the word fish, you can help them first to split the spoken word 'fish' into all the different sounds that it contains: 'f', 'i' and 'sh'.

Then you can help them to remember which letters are used to represent those sounds: f, i and sh and to write those letters down in order: fish.

How words are built – vowels and consonants
Spoken words are built using **vowel sounds** and **consonant sounds**.

Vowel sounds

Vowel sounds are 'open' sounds – the sounds that we make without blocking air with our lips, teeth or tongue.
Vowel sounds are represented by the letters **a, e, i, o, u** and sometimes **y**.
Some vowel sounds use a combination of these and other letters, e.g.
a, e, i, o, u, y, ai, ee, ou, oo, ee, a-e, igh, eigh, aigh.

Consonant sounds

Consonant sounds are 'closed' sounds – sounds that we make by blocking air with our lips, teeth or tongue.

Consonant sounds are represented by all of the other letters in the alphabet, and by combinations of consonants, e.g.

s, **t**, **p**, **n**, **ch**, **ck**, **sh**, **th**, **tch**.

Easy words and hard words

Your child will hear sounds most clearly, and read and spell words most easily, when consonant sounds are separated by vowel sounds:

i t

vowel consonant

c a t

consonant vowel consonant

sh i p

consonant vowel consonant

The order in which words are introduced

Your child will first be shown words that are easiest to read and spell and then, gradually, more difficult word structures are introduced.

1. Short, simple words

Children are first introduced to written words that have just one consonant sound and one vowel sound, e.g. **to**, **do**, **in**, **at**.

These are known as **CV words** (consonant/vowel) and **VC words** (vowel/**consonant**).

At the same time, they are also introduced to words that have a consonant, then a vowel and then a consonant. These are known as CVC words. Here are some examples:

cat	c a t
mum	m u m
chip	ch i p
fish	f i sh

2. Longer simple words

Next children are introduced to simple words with two syllables. Simple two syllable words are those in which all the consonant sounds are separated by vowel sounds. Here are some examples:

rabbit	r a bb i t
robin	r o b i n
ladder	ch i p

TERMINOLOGY

Syllable:
a beat in a word, e.g.
do (one syllable),
undo (two syllables),
undoing (three syllables)

3. Short, complex words

Then children are introduced to words that have two consonants at the beginning or end. These are known as **CCVC words** and **CVCC words**. Here are some examples:

s t ee **p**   **s p** i n

s p e **ck**   m e **n d**

b e **n t**   t e **n th**

Where possible, we can first introduce these CCVC words and CVCC words by showing how they can be made by building on CVC words:

t o p $\longrightarrow$ **s** t o p

m e n $\longrightarrow$ m e n **d**

Some of these strings of consonants sounds are found together in words a lot, so children are introduced to them, and to sets of words that contain them:

pl	st	bl	cr	nt
play	**st**op	**bl**ack	**cr**y	tent
plod	**st**and	**bl**ow	**cr**isp	ant
plan	po**st**	**bl**ink	**cr**unch	sent

These consonant strings are sometimes known as **consonant clusters**. When introducing consonant clusters, we need to be sure that children can still identify each individual sound, as well as the string of sounds that they make together.

TERMINOLOGY

consonant cluster:
A group of consonants that appear next to each other in a word, but that all keep their separate sounds, e.g. play, stroke, ask, band.

4. Longer complex words

The next step is to introduce children to words with consonant clusters at both ends – **CCVCC words** – and to consonant clusters with three consonant sounds in a row – **CCCVC and CCCVCC words**. Here are some examples:

s t a **n d**   **s t r** ee t

th r u **s t**   **s c r** u **n ch**

They are also introduced to two-syllable words that have consonant clusters at this stage. Here's an example:

t w i **s t** i ng

Tricky words and non-phonics based methods

In some words that your child will use every day, the match between the letters and the sounds is unusual:

e.g. **no   the   to   was   who**

These words are sometimes called 'tricky words'. Your child may also find other words difficult, even when the letters and sounds do fit a common pattern.

With these tricky or difficult words, phonic games and approaches – helping children to identify and remember which letters represent which sounds – still need to be the key methods used. However, we can add to the phonic games and activities with the following additional approaches.

Multi-sensory approaches

Many children learn and remember better if learning involves feeling or doing, as well as hearing or seeing.

Touching and holding things that they are learning about, feeling things on their skin, running, walking or moving their bodies in other ways, and even tasting or smelling things can all help your child to learn and remember.

Wordplay
Silly sentences made from the letters in a word can help your child remember the spelling, e.g. **B**ig **E**lephants **C**an **A**lways **U**nderstand **S**mall **E**lephants (***because***).

Highlighting common word parts

There are some longer word parts that are used frequently in English. You can point these out to your child, particularly where the sounds made by the letters are unusual, e.g. **ture**: pic**ture**, adven**ture**, furni**ture**.

Handwriting approaches

Writing a word with a smooth, regular movement may help your child to remember it, particularly if they use joined-up handwriting.

Understanding word parts

Words can often be split into different word parts. Learning about the meaning or effect of different word parts can help your child to remember how to spell them, even when the sounds change. Here's an example:

Add '**ed**' *if it happened in the past.* 'I **walk** every day' becomes 'I **walked** yesterday'.

Other words that follow this pattern include **push** and **post**.

For a list of word parts that can be added to the ends of words to change the meaning, see the list of suffixes on page 94.

Look, say, trace, cover, write

With this method, your child looks closely at a word and the graphemes that make it, saying and tracing the **graphemes**, then covering and trying to write the word. Your child repeats this a few times a week. Words with the same pattern can be practised together, e.g. The c**ou**ple of y**ou**ng c**ou**sins were d**ou**ble tr**ou**ble. For a full explanation of this method, see page 87.

Word	Tip	Write and trace	Try 1	Try 2
couple	c **ou** p **le**	couple	couple	couple
cousins	c **ou** s i n s			
double	d **ou** b **le**			
trouble	t r **ou** b **le**			

Rules

Spelling rules are attempts to describe patterns in English spelling. An example is '**i** before **e** except after **c**', as in the words **fri**end and re**cei**ve.

Rules are often complicated and frequently have exceptions. Consider the word **an**ci**e**nt, for example.

Many children find rules hard to remember. However, your child may sometimes find that rules are useful ways to back up, or reinforce, other methods of learning.

TERMINOLOGY

Grapheme:
a letter or group of letters that represents one sound, e.g. sh, t or ck

Most of the games in this book include approaches such as these, alongside phonics, to help your child learn. In the section 'Further games for tricky or difficult words', on page 80, these additional approaches are the main focus.

How to choose and use the games

If you're not sure how to choose a game for your child, or which sounds, letters or words to practise once you've chosen a game, here are some tips:

1. Look again at the chart 'Steps for developing phonics skills:'

Steps for developing phonics skills	Pages for games
1. Hearing individual sounds	29
2. Hearing individual sounds in words	34
3. Splitting spoken words into sounds and blending sounds into spoken words	40
Then, cycles of:	
4. Matching sounds and letters	47
5. Reading or spelling words	60
Alongside this, children are also shown:	
6. Additional non-phonic methods for reading and spelling tricky words	80

Steps 1, 2 and 3 develop the close listening skills that your child needs before they read or write letters and words. Steps 4, 5, and 6 help your child to develop the skills needed to read or write letters and words. Even if your child has started to read and write letters and words, they may still benefit from improving their listening skills with games from the first three stages.

2. Think about what stage your child needs to practise
If you're not sure, you can ask your child's school, pre-school or nursery staff. Or, you can try a game from an early section and see whether your child finds it easy or hard, fun or boring.

3. Use the column 'Pages for games' to find the right games for your child's level of development

TERMINOLOGY

Grapheme:
*a letter or group of
letters that represents
one sound, e.g.* sh, t
or ck

Choosing which *sounds* or phonemes **to focus on:**

If you want your child to practise hearing individual sounds on their own or in words, and you're not sure which sounds to focus on, use the list of **graphemes** on pages 89-93, to help you. You can start at the beginning of the list, focusing on the sounds represented by the first letters. If your child already knows some of the sounds that these letters represent, then gradually build in a few of the new ones that come next in the list.

Choosing which *letters* or graphemes **to focus on:**

If you want your child to practise matching sounds and letters, and you're not sure which letters and sounds to focus on, use the list of **graphemes** on pages 89-93, to help you. You could start at the beginning of the list or, if your child already knows some letters and the sounds they represent, start with a few of those that they know, then gradually introduce new ones that come next in the list.

Choosing which *words* to focus on:

If you're reading and spelling words and need help choosing words to focus on, see the list of **graphemes**, with its accompanying list of words, on pages 89-93. You could start with the words that match the graphemes at the beginning of the list. Alternatively, if your child can already read or spell some words, introduce new words by finding the first grapheme in the list that they have not yet practised reading or spelling in words. Use the group of words that comes with that grapheme.

Helping with words and graphemes that your child *finds tricky:*

If the graphemes or words that your child is learning are tricky, or your child is finding them particularly hard, you can add to the phonics games with games from the section 'Further games for reading and spelling tricky or difficult words' on pages 80-86.

Games for hearing sounds

WHAT'S IN THE BOX?

What's the game?

This fun guessing game helps your child to listen to sounds carefully, in preparation for matching sounds to letters for reading and spelling. When strange, mystery noises come from a box, your child listens hard to each noise and tries to guess what objects are making them.

You will need

➡ A few objects that can make a noise, e.g. keys, a balloon, a plastic bag, a clock, a whistle, a rubber band, a handful of pasta shells, a box of matches.

➡ A box to hide all the objects in.

How to play ➡➡➡➡➡➡➡➡➡➡➡➡➡➡➡➡➡➡➡➡➡➡➡

1. Hold the box so that your child cannot see what object you are holding.

2. Choose an object and, keeping it hidden, make a noise with it.

3. Ask your child to guess what the object is. Repeat with different objects.

Make it easier...

✸ Show your child all the objects first. Then hide them, make a noise with one and ask your child to guess which of the objects is making the noise.

✸ Show your child all the objects first and also show each object making a noise. Then hide them, make a noise with one and ask your child to remember which object made that noise.

29

OUR KITCHEN BAND

What's the game?

Banging on pots and pans is fun. This game helps your child to listen carefully to tricky noise patterns, preparing them for hearing all of the sounds in words and matching them to letters, for spelling and reading.

You will need

➡ A few kitchen utensils that can make a noise, e.g. metal spoons, metal pans, wooden spoons, a cheese grater, a colander.

How to play ➡ ➡ ➡ ➡ ➡

1 Make a simple tune with the utensils.

2 Ask your child to copy your tune.

Make it harder...

✹ Ask your child to turn around so that they can't see you when you play a simple tune. Now ask them to play back to you the tune that they heard you play.

MIRROR MY SOUND SONG

What's the game?

Singing and copying sound patterns is a great way for your child to prepare for identifying the different sounds in words and matching them to letters, for spelling and reading.

You will need

➡ Have in mind a song or nursery rhyme that your child enjoys.

➡ Choose a sound/phoneme for your child to practise listening to and copying. If you'd like help choosing which phoneme to focus on, go to the chapter 'How to choose and use the games', page 28.

How to play ➡➡➡➡➡➡➡➡➡➡➡➡➡➡➡➡➡➡➡➡➡➡➡➡

1 Choose a part of the song that your child knows well and swap the words for the phoneme you have chosen, repeating the phoneme to fit the rhythm of the song. E.g., replace the syllables of the song '1, 2, 3, 4, 5, once I caught a fish alive' with 'sh, sh, sh, sh, sh, sh sh sh sh sh sh-sh'.

2 Sing your phoneme tune to your child. Ask them to sing it back to you.

Add a twist

Add some fun or silly dance moves for your child to copy too.

TOP TIP:
Pronouncing sounds clearly can be tricky for adults. See the 'How to...' box on page 13 for help.

Make it harder...

✹ Use two or three different phonemes to swap with the words of the song. Can your child copy the phoneme pattern you have made?

✹ Try saying the phoneme pattern without a familiar tune. Can your child still remember and repeat the pattern you have made?

STORY SOUND EFFECTS

What's the game?
Children can learn lots from their favourite stories. This game helps your child to listen closely to words and to sound patterns, developing their understanding as well as preparing them for matching sounds to letters for reading and spelling words. Your child copies or makes sound effects for a story.

You will need
➡ A story that your child will enjoy, to which you can add sound effects.

Before you play
★ Plan some sound effects that you could add to the story. For example, you could add the sounds of animals ('moo'), vehicles ('vrrooom'), rain (pitta-patta, pitta-patta), wind ('shwwooo'), laughing ('ha ha ha ha!') or crying ('boo hoo hoo'). If you can, choose sounds that can be repeated a few times through the story.

How to play ➡➡➡➡➡➡➡➡➡➡➡➡➡➡➡➡➡➡➡➡➡➡

1. Read or tell the story to your child. Include all of the sound effects. Ask your child to join in by copying the sound effects when you make them.

2. The next time you tell the story, can your child join in with the sound effects straight away?

Make it harder...

✹ When you next tell the story, see whether your child can remember where the sound effects go, and what sounds to make, before you remind them.

✹ Ask your child to make their own sound effect for a part of the story. Can they remember to include their sound effect next time you read the story?

THE WHISPER CHAIN

What's the game?

Silly sounds are always funny and silly mistakes are even funnier. This game includes both! You'll need a few people to join in. Those playing whisper a string of silly sounds from one person to the next. Will the sound string be the same at the end of the chain as it was at the beginning? Careful listening to sound strings will help your child prepare for reading and spelling words.

You will need

➡ A few children.

How to play ➡➡➡➡➡➡➡➡➡➡➡➡➡➡➡➡➡➡➡➡➡➡➡➡

1 Ask the children to stand or sit in a line.

2 Ask the first child in the line to think of a short string of sounds and whisper it to the next child.

3 The sound string is then whispered from child to child along the line.

4 The last child says out loud the sound string they have heard. Has it changed?

Make it easier...

✳ You can start with real words instead of random sounds, as they will be easier to remember. For example, the first child can give a string of fruit names or animal names: 'dog, cat, mouse, duck'.

Games for hearing sounds in words

FIND ME A MATCH

What's the game?

This game helps your child to identify sounds in words, in preparation for matching sounds to letters for reading and spelling words. Your child chooses an object to match a sound that you make. The funnier the objects, the better the game! Can you get any family members or pets to join in?

You will need

➡ Have in mind a few sounds or **phonemes** that your child is ready to practise. If you'd like some help choosing which phonemes to focus on, go to the chapter 'How to choose and use the games', page 28.

➡ A few household objects, people, animals or toys whose names start with those phonemes.

How to play ➡➡➡➡➡➡➡➡➡➡➡➡➡➡➡➡➡➡➡➡➡➡➡

1 Show your child the objects you have gathered.

2 Say a phoneme and ask your child to find the object that starts with that phoneme.

Make it harder...

✸ Say a phoneme that none of your objects start with. Ask your child to find an object in the room or house that starts with that phoneme.

✸ Say a phoneme and ask your child to choose an object that has that phoneme at the end or in the middle of its name.

WHERE'S THE PAIR?

What's the game?

In this game, your child matches together pairs of objects that start with the same sound. This game helps your child to identify and match sounds in words, preparing them for matching sounds to letters for reading and spelling words. Include some silly objects or treats to add to the fun!

You will need

➡ A few household objects or toys.

How to play ⇨⇨⇨⇨⇨⇨⇨⇨⇨⇨⇨⇨⇨⇨⇨⇨⇨⇨⇨⇨⇨⇨⇨⇨

1 Collect a group of objects that includes pairs of objects that start with the same sound, e.g. bat/ball, pear/pot, chocolate/chalk.

2 Ask your child to match together the objects that start with the same sound.

3 Can your child then tell you what each of the matching sounds are?

Add a twist

Give your child a few seconds to look at the objects then hide them away under a tea towel. Can they remember any that start with the same sound?

TOP TIP:

Pronouncing sounds clearly can be tricky for adults. See the 'How to...' box on page 13 for help.

Make it harder...

✳ Ask your child to match objects with names that have the same phonemes at the end or in the middle, e.g. cat/pot, boot/spoon.

SNEAKY SOUND SETS

What's the game?

Building on the previous game, 'Where's the pair?', this game helps your child fine-tune their skills at identifying sounds, by using groups of objects that start with similar, easily confused sounds. This prepares your child for matching similar sounds to the right letters when reading and spelling words.

You will need

➡ A few household objects or toys, some that start with exactly the same sound and some that start with a similar but slightly different sound. For example, you can gather some objects that begin with 'sh' and some other objects that begin with 's'.

How to play ➡➡➡➡➡➡➡➡➡➡➡➡➡➡➡➡➡➡➡➡➡➡➡

1. Show your child the objects you have collected.

2. Can your child sort the objects into sets of objects that start with the same sound?

3. Can your child tell you the sound that each set begins with?

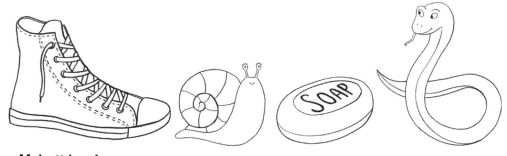

Make it harder...

* Can your child think of other things that start with either of the sounds? Can they tell you which set of things they would go in?

* Find other objects. Can your child tell whether each new object can be added to one of the sets or needs a whole new set?

MY SOUNDS SCRAPBOOK

What's the game?

Lots of children love to make their very own book. In this game, you and your child make a sounds scrapbook. This helps your child to identify and match the sounds in words, preparing them for matching sounds to the letters when reading and spelling words.

You will need

➡ A blank scrapbook, pictures (from magazines, internet, etc.) and/or paper, pencils or pens.

➡ Have in mind which sounds to start with. You could start with phonemes that your child uses a lot, such as the first sound in their name. If you'd like some help choosing which phonemes to focus on, go to the chapter 'How to choose and use the games', page 28.

How to play ➡

1 Together with your child, make a scrapbook of pictures. On each double page, focus on things that begin with the same sound.

2 You could start things off with a picture of a person or thing that begins with a familiar sound. It could even be a picture of your child.

3 Can your child think of other things that start with the same sound? Together, can you find or draw pictures of things that start with that sound? You could use pictures from magazines, the internet or food wrappers, or your child could draw their own pictures – this is especially fun for budding little artists.

Make it harder...

✳ Choose a new sound to focus on. Can your child think of some things that start with that sound without any help from you? Can they find or draw the pictures on their own?

✳ When you have covered a few sounds, gather a selection of pictures. Can your child add any of them to the pages they have already made?

FUN PHONICS SHOPPING

What's the game?

In this game, you and your child make a silly shopping list in which everything starts with the same sound. It's surprising what you can find at the shops sometimes! This game helps your child to identify and match individual sounds.

You will need

➡ Choose which sound to start with. If you'd like some help choosing which phonemes to focus on, go to the chapter 'How to choose and use the games', on page 27. Find the section 'Choosing which sounds or phonemes to focus on'.

How to play ➡➡➡➡➡➡➡➡➡➡➡➡➡➡➡➡➡➡➡➡➡➡

1 Tell your child that you are going to the shops but everything you buy must start with the same sound, e.g. **p**orridge, **p**ig.

2 Start the shopping list and see whether they can add more items starting with the same sound.

Make it harder...

* Can your child choose a sound and make a shopping list on their own?

Add a twist

Take it in turns to add a new item to the list and to repeat the whole shopping list. How long can your child keep going, remembering every item on the shopping list?

SAME SOUND SONJA AND SIMON

What's the game?

In this game the only limit is your child's imagination, as they describe imaginary objects using words that each start with the same sound. This game helps your child to identify and match individual sounds in words, preparing them for matching sounds and letters for reading and spelling words.

You will need

➡ A few household objects or toys.

How to play ➡➡➡➡➡➡➡➡➡➡➡➡➡➡➡➡➡➡➡➡➡➡➡➡

1 Tell your child about Same Sound Sonja and Simon, who make up funny descriptions in which all, or most of, the words start with the same sound.

2 Give your child an object and ask them to imagine another one of the same thing, which they can describe with a few words that all start with the same sound. Such as a 'huge, hard hat' and a 'horrible, hairy hat'.

Make it easier...

✸ You can start with your own funny description of an object and see whether your child can add another word. For example, you could say a 'huge, hard hat', and your child can add another adjective such as 'heavy'.

Add a twist

Instead of focusing on objects, add real or made-up words to people's names: *'Boo Bop Bonnie'*, *'Mega Marvellous Maia'*, etc.

Games for splitting spoken words into sounds

and blending sounds into spoken words

SOUNDS INTO WORDS; WORDS INTO SOUNDS

What's the game?

In this guessing game, your child blends spoken sounds together to find the names of objects. They also split spoken words into individual sounds. This prepares your child for blending sounds for reading and splitting words for spelling.

How to play ➡

1 Place all of the objects or pictures together on a table or the floor.

2 You secretly choose an object.

3 Split the object's name into all the separate sounds and say them out loud. For example: 's – o – ck'. Can your child identify which object you are naming?

4 Try with another object.

5 Now, can your child split the name of an object for you to guess?

Make it harder...

✹ Start with the objects hidden in a box. Can your child guess the objects from you saying the separate sounds without seeing them first?

's' 'o' 'ck'

WORD CHAIN

What's the game?

In this game, you and your child change spoken words, one sound at a time, to make some new spoken words. How many new words can you make? This game helps your child to hear individual sounds, blend sounds into words and split words into sounds. This prepares them for blending sounds into words for reading and splitting words for spelling.

You will need

➡ A few objects or pictures of things with names that are short, simple words – **CVC words**. For a list of common CVC words, see the words highlighted in **bold** in the Word Lists on pages 89-93.

How to play ➡➡➡➡➡➡➡➡➡➡➡➡➡➡➡➡➡➡➡➡➡➡➡

1 Ask your child to pick an object and to say its name.
For example, 'pig'.

2 You split the name into the separate sounds: p-i-g.

3 Now you change just one sound to make a new word: b-i-g. Big.

4 Ask your child to change one sound of your new word to make another new word. For example, 'big' could become 'b-i-t. Bit.' If this is hard, they can make non-words too. Help them to just change one sound at a time.

Make it harder...

❋ Start with a new word. This time, see whether your child can split it into separate sounds and be the first to change a sound to make a new word.

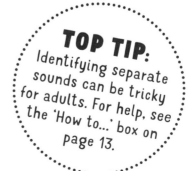

TOP TIP:
Identifying separate sounds can be tricky for adults. For help, see the 'How to...' box on page 13.

SING THE SOUNDS

What's the game?

This game can be played at any time and in any place. Your child splits familiar spoken words into sounds, preparing them for splitting spoken words into sounds for spelling, and also for blending sounds into words for reading.

You will need

➡ Just your imagination.

How to play ➡➡➡➡➡➡➡➡➡➡➡➡➡➡➡➡➡➡➡➡➡➡

1 Notice sentences with a short, simple key word (ideally a **CVC word**) that you use a lot, such as 'cat' (c-a-t) or 'shop' (sh-o-p).

2 Whenever you use one of the sentences, sing it out, splitting the key word into individual sounds. Clapping to the sounds will help them stand out even more.

3 Encourage your child to join in.

'We're going to the sh-o-p'

Make it harder...

✹ Once your child has become familiar with your special sentence, when you next start the sentence, can they finish it on their own, remembering how to split the key word?

✹ Find another simple key word that you use a lot. Can your child split the word into sounds themselves, without your help?

✹ Choose a slightly longer word – for example a word containing a consonant cluster: 'We love to p – l – ay!'

ISLAND HOPPING

What's the game?

In this game, imaginary dangers and physical activity add excitement and help learning. Your child blends spoken sounds into words, and splits spoken words into sounds, preparing them for blending sounds into words for reading and splitting words into sounds for spelling.

You will need

➡ A few objects with names that are short, simple words (for a list of common short, simple words, see the Word List on page 89).

➡ A box.

➡ Some sheets of paper cut to look island-shaped.

Before you play

★ Choose a room or open space to play. Identify a 'home area' on one side, such as a chair or cushion, to represent the mainland.

★ Spread the sheets of paper across the space, each about 50 cm apart, so that they end at the home area/'mainland'.

★ Hide your objects in the box.

How to play ➡➡➡➡➡➡➡➡➡➡➡➡➡➡➡➡➡➡➡➡➡➡➡

1 Start at the paper island furthest from the 'mainland'. Explain to your child that they are stranded and must hop from island to island to reach the safety of the mainland.

2 Tell your child that they must leave a gift at each island before moving on. Say that you have the gifts hidden and they can have them if they guess the names from your sound clues.

3 At the first island, sound out the name of one of the objects in your box, phoneme by phoneme (e.g. 'p – a – n'). If your child can name the object correctly, give them the object to leave on the 'island' and tell them to hop to the next island.

4 Continue with the name guessing and island hopping until your child reaches the 'mainland'.

Add a twist
This time, put an object on each of the islands. Explain that your child can only move on to the next island if they can split the name of the object into all its separate sounds (e.g. 's – o – ck').

THE BIG, BOLD ACTION BLEND

What's the game?

Here's another game with movement and lots of room for silliness. In this game, your child blends sounds together to work out key words in sets of instructions.

You will need

➡ Just your imagination.

How to play ➡➡➡➡➡➡➡➡➡➡➡➡➡➡➡➡➡➡➡➡➡➡➡➡

1 Give your child simple instructions for an action to do, but split a simple key word in the instructions. E.g. 'P – a – t your head' or 'R – u – b your tummy'.

2 See whether your child can follow your instructions.

3 Can your child give you an instruction with a split word in it?

* Make it harder...
Split a few words in the instruction and/or split a word that is a bit harder:
'T – ou – ch the f – l – oo – r'.

Games for matching sounds and letters

MATCH THE LETTER

What's the game?

In this simple game, your child matches letters, or letter groups, to sounds, building this key skill for reading and spelling.

You will need

➡ A few household objects or toys.

➡ Blank **flashcards** and pencil or pen.

➡ Have in mind two or three **graphemes** - letters or groups of letters that represent one sound - for your child to practise. If you'd like some help choosing which graphemes to focus on, go to the Word Lists on pages 88-93. Start at the beginning of the list, and if your child already knows some of the sounds, gradually add new ones.

How to play ➡ ➡ ➡ ➡ ➡

1. Pick two or three different graphemes for your child to practise. Write them onto **flashcards**. Discuss and practise their sounds with your child.

2. Say a sound matching one of the graphemes. Ask your child to hold up the correct grapheme.

Make it harder...

✺ Say a whole word and ask your child to hold up the grapheme that it starts with.

Make it harder STILL...

✺ Hold up an object or toy that starts with one of the graphemes. Ask your child to hold up the grapheme that it starts with.

✺ Ask your child to hold up a grapheme that is at the **end** of the name of an object.

Add a twist

Ask your child to choose one of the graphemes and then find an object in the room that starts with it.

PERFECT PAIRS

What's the game?

In this pairing game, your child matches letters to objects or pictures. This helps them to build the key skill of matching letters to sounds for reading and spelling.

You will need

➡ Some **flashcards**, with a few **graphemes** written on them for your child to practise. If you'd like some help choosing which graphemes to focus on, go to the Word Lists on pages 88-93.

➡ Some objects, or pictures of things, with names in which the first sounds match the grapheme flashcards.

How to play ➡➡➡➡➡➡➡➡➡➡➡➡➡➡➡➡➡➡➡➡➡➡➡➡

1️⃣ Ask your child to match the graphemes with the objects or pictures.

2️⃣ If needed, you can help by first discussing the names of the objects or pictures and also practising the sounds made by the graphemes.

Add a twist

Can your child find more objects that will match any of the flashcards?

Make it harder...

✱ If you take away one of the flashcards, can your child write the grapheme from memory onto a blank flashcard?

48

LOVELY LARGE LETTERS

What's the game?

In this big movement game, your child traces and draws huge letters and remembers the sounds that they represent, preparing them for matching letters to sounds for reading and spelling.

You will need

➡ A tool to trace or draw huge letters – e.g. a mop, chalk, marker pen or wand.

➡ Have in mind a few **graphemes** for your child to practise. If you'd like some help choosing which graphemes to focus on, go to the Word Lists on pages 88-93.

How to play ➡➡➡➡➡➡➡➡➡➡➡➡➡➡➡➡➡➡➡➡➡➡➡➡

1 Choose a tool that you and your child can use to write or trace huge letters. For example, they can use a mop on a floor, chalk on a concrete path, a marker pen on a huge sheet of paper or a wand/streamer for air writing.

2 Draw a big **grapheme** and see whether your child can remember the sound that it represents.

3 Ask your child to trace the grapheme and then to draw it themselves.

Make it harder...

✹ Instead of drawing a grapheme yourself, say a single sound – **phoneme** – and see whether your child can draw the grapheme that represents it.

MAKING GRAPHEMES

What's the game?

In this craft game, your child uses modelling clay to make letters to match sounds. Remembering the shapes of the letters that match a sound, and then making that shape, builds key skills for reading and spelling.

You will need

➡ Some modelling clay or salt dough.

➡ Have in mind a few **graphemes** for your child to practise. If you'd like some help choosing which graphemes to focus on, go to the Word Lists on pages 88-93.

How to play ⇨

1 Say the sound represented by the grapheme you have in mind.

2 Can your child make the grapheme out of modelling clay?

Make it easier...

✸ If your child can't remember the letter, or letters, that matches the sound that you have made, draw the letter for them, and then ask them to make it with their modelling clay.

Make it harder...

✸ Instead of saying a sound, say a whole word and see whether your child can make a grapheme to match the first sound in the word.

✸ Show your child an object and see whether they can make the grapheme that matches the first sound in its name.

✸ Say a word and see whether your child can make a grapheme to match the sound at the **end** of the word.

TERRIBLE TICKLY LETTERS

What's the game?

If your child likes to be tickled, they'll love this game. It uses the sense of touch to help your child learn and remember the shapes of letters, and the sounds that those letters represent. Your child feels letters being traced on their arm and recalls the sound that the letters represent.

You will need

➡ A soft, clean paintbrush.

➡ Have in mind a few **graphemes** for your child to practise. If you'd like some help choosing which graphemes to focus on, go to the Word Lists on pages 88-93.

How to play ➡➡➡➡➡➡➡➡➡➡➡➡➡➡➡➡➡➡➡➡➡➡➡➡➡

1 Ask your child to close their eyes. Gently trace the grapheme you have chosen onto your child's arm.

2 Can your child say the phoneme represented by the grapheme you are tracing?

Add a twist

Let your child trace a grapheme onto your arm. See whether you can say the phoneme represented by it. Can your child tell whether you are right or wrong?

LETTERS OF THE WEEK

What's the game?

Making their very own book helps your child to match letters to sounds in words, in preparation for matching letters to sounds for reading and spelling. Your child can focus on one letter or letter group each week, finding or making pictures for a letter scrapbook.

You will need

➡ A blank scrapbook, some pictures (from magazines, internet, etc.), paper and pens or pencils.

➡ Have in mind some letters **graphemes** for your child to learn. If you'd like some help choosing which graphemes to focus on, go to the Word Lists on pages 88-93.

How to play ⇨

1 Choose a grapheme to start with and say the sound that it represents to your child. Write the grapheme lightly on a piece of paper. Ask your child to draw over your version of the grapheme, or to copy it onto their own piece of paper.

2 Stick the grapheme onto a fresh page of the scrapbook. Encourage your child to gather or draw pictures of objects whose names start with that grapheme.

3 Throughout the week, see how many objects your child can spot which begin with that grapheme. They could also look out for objects, or pictures of things, which have that grapheme in the middle or at the end.

Add a twist

Instead of writing graphemes with a pen or pencil, write them with glue and then sprinkle sand, sequins or glitter over the glue. Now your child can feel the letters as well as see them.

WRITE THE LETTER

What's the game?

In this game, your child writes letters to match the first sounds of objects' names, building key skills for spelling. Use objects that are silly, interesting or yummy to add to the fun of this game!

You will need

➡ A few household objects or toys, some paper and a pencil or pen.

➡ Have in mind some **graphemes** for your child to learn. If you'd like some help choosing which graphemes to focus on, go to the Word Lists on pages 88-93.

How to play ➡

1 Find some household objects that have the chosen graphemes at the beginning of their names. The sillier the objects the better!

2 Give your child some pieces of paper and a pencil or pen.

3 Hold up an object and see whether your child can write down the grapheme that it starts with.

Make it easier...

✱ Choose a few objects that all start with one of two graphemes. You draw the grapheme for the first one of the set, and then ask your child to do the rest.

Make it harder...

✱ Choose some objects that have graphemes at the **end** of their names that your child is ready to practise.

Add a twist

Ask your child to choose a grapheme that they know how to write and say. Hold up an object and ask your child to decide whether it matches their chosen grapheme.

HIDDEN LETTERS

What's the game?

Children love having secrets. In this game, your child writes a letter or group of letters, hides it and gives clues to help you guess what it is. Writing letters and matching them to sounds in words are key skills for reading and spelling.

You will need

➡ A few household objects or toys, some paper and a pencil or pen.

➡ Have in mind some **graphemes** for your child to learn. If you'd like some help choosing which graphemes to focus on, go to the Word Lists on pages 88-93.

How to play ➡➡➡➡➡➡➡➡➡➡➡➡➡➡➡➡➡➡➡➡➡

1 Ask your child to choose a grapheme that they know how to write and say. Tell them to write it on a piece of paper, fold the paper away and keep the grapheme secret.

2 Now, can they draw or find an object that starts with that grapheme, to help you guess it?

Make it easier...

✳ If your child finds this a bit hard, you can write and hide the grapheme, and draw or find clues to help them guess.

✳ Alternatively, you can write a few graphemes on separate pieces of paper and then ask them to secretly select one and find clues to help you guess which one they have chosen.

54

LISTEN CLOSE

What's the game?

In this game, your child fine-tunes their skills at identifying sounds and matching them to letters. They listen carefully to hear the difference between sounds that are often mixed up and then match those sounds to the right letters. This is great practice for matching easily confused sounds to the right letters when reading and spelling.

You will need

➡ Two large, blank flashcards.

➡ Have in mind a sound that your child sometimes muddles with a similar but different sound. (Some commonly muddled sounds are those represented by the letters **f** and **th**, **v** and **f**, or **zz** and **s**.)

How to play ➡

1 Write the two different letters or letter groups – graphemes – that represent the easily muddled sounds onto the blank flashcards and give them to your child.

2 Say a word with one of the sounds in it. If necessary, exaggerate the pronunciation of the key sound so that your child can hear it clearly.

3 Ask your child to hold up the grapheme that matches a sound in your word.

4 Try again with a different word.

Make it harder...

✳ Instead of saying aloud a word that starts with one of the sounds, hold up an object, or picture of an object, that starts with one of the sounds.

THE GRAPHEME TWIST

What's the game?

In this game, your child is only a wobble away from collapsing on the floor in a heap of giggles as they stretch and turn to reach letters that match the sounds that you make. Hearing sounds and identifying the letters that represent them is a key skill for spelling and reading.

You will need

➡ Paper and pens or pencils. Optional: some sticky tac.

➡ Have in mind some **graphemes** for your child to practise using. If you'd like some help choosing which graphemes to focus on, go to the Word Lists on pages 88-93.

How to play ➡➡➡➡➡➡➡➡➡➡➡➡➡➡➡➡➡➡➡➡➡➡

① Choose six graphemes that your child is ready to practise using. Write them on separate sheets of paper. Place them on the floor a little apart. You can keep them in place with sticky tac.

② Say a sound and ask your child to place a foot or a hand on the grapheme that represents it.

③ Say another sound. Can your child place a different foot or hand on the grapheme that represents this new sound, without moving the foot or hand already in place?

④ Keep going until you have said four sounds. Has your child tumbled over yet?!

Make it harder...

✸ Say a whole word instead. Can your child identify the sound at the beginning, end (harder still) or middle (even harder) and then find the right grapheme?

Add a twist
Tell your child which hand or foot they have to place on the correct grapheme. How much twisting will you make them do?!

TOP TIP:
Start with graphemes that represent quite different phonemes. As your child's knowledge of graphemes develops, choose graphemes such as **th**, **sh** and **f** that represent quite similar sounds. See whether your child can still identify the right grapheme.

THE GRAPHEME MONSTER CHASE

What's the game?

In this game, your child follows a paper path to escape a monster, but they must say the sounds represented by letters on each piece of paper before they can move on. Remembering the sounds represented by letters is a key skill for reading.

You will need

➡ Paper and pens or pencils. Optional: some sticky tac.

➡ Have in mind some **graphemes** for your child to practise using. If you'd like some help choosing which graphemes to focus on, go to the Word Lists on pages 88-93.

How to play ➡➡➡➡➡➡➡➡➡➡➡➡➡➡➡➡➡➡➡➡➡➡➡➡

1 Write a few of your chosen graphemes on separate sheets of paper. Place them on the floor a little apart. You can keep them in place with sticky tac.

2 Tell your child that the paper path is the only way to escape the terrible monster that is chasing them, but they can only move from one piece of paper to the next if they can read the graphemes on the paper.

3 Start chasing!

Make it harder...

✱ Ask your child to read each grapheme and then to say a word that includes that grapheme before moving on.

THE GRAPHEME STEPPING STONES

What's the game?

In this game, your child uses paper stepping stones to cross a raging river, but they must write letters for the sounds they hear onto each stepping stone before they are able to move on. Remembering and drawing the letters that represent different sounds are key skills for spelling.

You will need

➡ Paper and pens or pencils. Optional: some sticky tac.

➡ Have in mind some **graphemes** for your child to practise using. If you'd like some help choosing which graphemes to focus on, go to the Word Lists on pages 88-93.

How to play ➡

1 Take a few sheets of paper. Place them on the floor a little apart. You can keep them in place with sticky tac.

2 Tell your child that each piece of paper is a stepping stone across a raging river, but that they will have to complete a task before they can move from one to the next.

3 Give your child a pen or pencil. Ask them to go to the first stepping stone. Say the sound represented by one of the chosen graphemes. Explain to your child that they must write the grapheme that represents that sound before they move on.

4 Now your child can move on to the next stepping stone and write another grapheme to match a sound that you say.

5 Keep going until they are safely across the river!

Make it harder...

✹ Ask your child to write a grapheme and then to say a word that includes that grapheme before moving on from each stepping stone.

Games for reading and spelling words

PLATE OF WORDS

What's the game?

In this game, word-building becomes a fun puzzle to solve. Your child builds words out of letters and groups of letters – great practice for reading and spelling words.

You will need

➡ A plate, blank **flashcards** and a pen or pencil.

➡ A group of words with a common **grapheme** that your child is ready to learn. If you'd like some help choosing which graphemes to focus on, go to the Word Lists on pages 88-93.

Before you play

★ Split a few of your chosen words into graphemes. Write each grapheme onto a flashcard. Write the common grapheme just once, putting it in a different colour so that it stands out.

★ Put the flashcards onto a plate.

How to play ➡➡➡➡➡➡➡➡➡➡➡➡➡➡➡➡➡➡➡➡➡➡➡➡➡

1 Ask your child to see how many words they can build with the flashcards.

2 Explain that the common grapheme needs to be in every word and that they can use each grapheme as many times as they like.

Make it easier...

* If your child can't see any words to build, start them off by saying a word that they can build. If they are still stuck, make the first word for them.

Make it harder...

* Replace some of the grapheme flashcards with blank flashcards. Can your child fill in the blank flashcards to build a word?

Make it harder STILL...

* Show your child the flashcards and ask them to look at them carefully, searching for any words that can be built. Now place a tea towel over the flashcards. How many of the words can your child remember? Can your child write any of them down?

THE SKITTLE ALLEY WORD BUILD

What's the game?

Here, a fun game of skittles becomes a great way for your child to practise building words for reading and spelling.

You will need

➡ A set of skittles (see **TOP TIP**), a ball, some blank **flashcards** and sticky tape or sticky tac.

➡ A group of words with a common **grapheme** your child is ready to practise. If you'd like some help choosing which graphemes to focus on, go to the Word Lists on pages 88-93.

Before you play

★ Split some of the chosen words into graphemes. Write the common grapheme onto a card and put it to one side. Write the other graphemes onto flashcards and stick them to the skittles. (Only write each grapheme once, even if it appears more than once in your words. Try to choose graphemes from which a few different words can be built.)

How to play ➡

1 Ask your child to throw the ball and see how many skittles they can knock down.

2 Give your child the flashcard with the common grapheme.

3 How many words can your child build using the common grapheme and the graphemes on the skittles that they knocked down? Each grapheme can be used as many times as needed.

Make it easier...

✳ If your child can't see any words to build, tell them a word that they can build. If they are still stuck, build the first word for them.

TOP TIP:
Empty plastic bottles make great skittles. You may want to put a little flour, sand or soil in the bottom of each so that they don't fall over **too** easily.

63

WORD MATCH

What's the game?

In this game, your child matches words to pictures or objects and then practises building those words, developing the skills needed for reading and spelling.

How to play ➡ ➡ ➡ ➡ ➡

(1) With the pencil, write words on the flashcards to match the pictures or objects.

(2) Ask your child to look at the pictures and say what they are.

(3) Now ask your child to read the words, sounding them out grapheme by grapheme with your help if needed.

(4) Can your child now match the words to the pictures?

Make it harder...

✳ With your child, carefully practise sounding out each grapheme in one of the words. Now, with the eraser, rub out the key grapheme in the word so that the paper looks something like this: g__l Can your child write the grapheme back in, to complete the word again?

✳ Next, rub out two graphemes in the same word. Can your child fill both graphemes in this time?

✳ Can your child now write the whole word by themselves?

Make it harder STILL...

✳ Can your child now make up and write (with help if needed) a sentence using as many of the words as possible, e.g.

The girl liked her shirt and skirt.

65

LOTS OF LOVELY LADDER WORDS

What's the game?

In this game, your child builds words by changing one letter, or group of letters, at a time. By remembering the sounds made by the letters and blending the sounds to make words, they are developing the key skills for reading.

You will need

➡ Three or four drawings or pictures of ladders, and a pen or pencil.

➡ A group of words with a common **grapheme** that your child is ready to practise. If you'd like some help choosing which graphemes to focus on, go to the Word Lists on pages 88–93.

Before you play

★ Split your words into **graphemes**. Write the grapheme that all your words have in the middle of one ladder. Write the other graphemes from your words between the rungs on the other ladder pictures.

How to play ➡

1. Place the ladders so that the central rungs line up.

2. Ask your child to read out the graphemes that are lined up and blend them together into a word. Can they tell whether it's a real word or a nonsense word?

3. Ask your child to choose a ladder and move it up or down one rung.

4. Can they read the new word? How many real words can they find altogether?

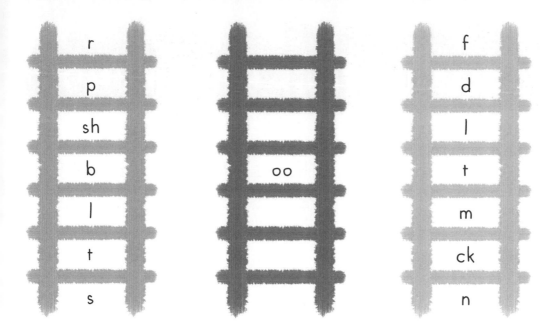

r
p
sh
b
l
t
s

oo

f
d
l
t
m
ck
n

Make it harder...

* Ask your child to make a sentence that includes some of the words that they have found.

* Can your child write another grapheme onto one of the ladders to build some new words?

LOLLIPOP STICK WORD BUILD

What's the game?

This lucky dip game gives an exciting twist to word-building. By reading letters and then blending them together to find words, your child practises the key skills needed for reading words. Some extra challenges help them to practise spelling skills too.

You will need

➡ Lolly sticks or other short sticks, blank **flashcards**, three or four bowls, some sand or flour, glue or sticky tape and a pen or pencil.

➡ A group of words with a common **grapheme** that your child is ready to practise. If you'd like some help choosing which graphemes to focus on, go to the Word Lists on pages 88-93.

Before you play

★ Split the words into graphemes. Write each grapheme onto a flashcard, with the common graphemes in a different colour.

★ Fix each flashcard onto a stick.

★ Push the sticks into the sand/flour bowls, so that the flashcards are buried. Put graphemes from the beginning of words together in the first bowl, those from the middle in the second bowl and those from the end in the third bowl.

How to play ➡

1 Ask your child to pick a stick from each bowl and to see whether they can build a word with the graphemes. They can swap the order if they wish.

2 If they can't build a word, they can return one of the sticks to its bowl and take another stick from the same bowl, and then try again.

Make it easier...

✸ If your child can't see a word to build with their graphemes, but there is one there, tell them the word and see whether they can build it.

Make it harder...

✸ Include some blank flashcards on the sticks. If your child picks a blank flashcard, can they write a grapheme on it that will complete a word with their other graphemes?

✸ How many of the words that they have already found can they recall and write down?

Add a twist
How many words can your child find in a set time?

69

BUILD WORDS ON PICTURES

What's the game?

In this art and craft game, your child builds words out of letters to complete a picture. By reading letters and blending the sounds together to find words, they are developing the skills they need for reading words. And, by writing their own letters to complete words, they are developing the key spelling skills too.

You will need

➡ A background picture that can be added to – for example, a tree without leaves, a train engine without carriages or an underwater scene without fish. Adults or children who enjoy art can make their own background picture, or pictures can be found online.

➡ Some **flashcards** in shapes to match the picture, such as leaves, train carriages or fish.

➡ A group of words with a common **grapheme** that your child is ready to practise. If you'd like some help choosing which graphemes to focus on, go to the Word Lists on pages 88-93.

How to play ➡➡➡➡➡➡➡➡➡➡➡➡➡➡➡➡➡➡➡➡➡➡

1 Split your words into graphemes and write each grapheme onto a separate flashcard.

2 Ask your child to finish the picture by building words with the flashcards.

Make it easier...

✹ Read the grapheme cards together before your child starts to build words.

✹ Before your child tries to build a word on their own, build one together, showing your child how they can read a grapheme and blend the sound with another and another to try to make a word.

Make it harder...

✹ Include some blank flashcards. Can your child still build words with the same common pattern, but writing one or two of the graphemes for themselves on the blank flashcards?

GRAPHEME STICK MAN

What's the game?

In this fun spelling game, your child splits words into sounds and remembers the letters that represent those sounds, developing key skills for spelling. But can they build a whole word before you have drawn a stick man?

You will need

➡ A pen or pencil and some blank paper.

➡ A group of words with a common **grapheme** that your child is ready to practise. If you'd like some help choosing which graphemes to focus on, go to the Word Lists on pages 88-93.

How to play ➡

1 Choose one of the words in the group for your child to try to spell. On the piece of paper, draw a line to represent each **grapheme** in the word.

2 Write the grapheme that's common to all of the words onto the appropriate line. For example, if your word was 'lamb' you might write:__ __ mb

3 Ask your child to think of another grapheme to add to the first one to start building a word, and to tell you the letter, or letters, it is made from.

4 If your child guesses a grapheme that is in your word, write it on the correct line. If the grapheme they offer is not in the word, draw the first line of a stick man.

5 Ask your child to keep guessing, with you adding correct graphemes to the word and adding lines to the stick man if they make incorrect guesses.

6 If your child completes the word before the stick man is complete, they have won. If not, you've won!

7 Try another word from the set.

Make it harder...
✳ Can your child remember a word from the set and lead the game for a round?

TOP TIP:
Do this a number of times and think about which words your child takes the longest to guess. Focus on the graphemes that make up these words in future games.

TWISTING TOWERS

What's the game?

In this game with tin cans, word-building becomes a fun physical activity. Your child twists and moves tin cans to build new words. Recognising and reading letters, then blending them together to find words, develops key reading skills. Choosing which letters to use and where to place them develops key spelling skills.

You will need

➡ Three to four groups of **CVC words**, each with a common **grapheme** that your child is ready to practise. For a list of common CVC words, see the words highlighted in bold in the Word Lists on pages 89-93.

➡ Five unopened food tins, a pen or pencil, some blank **flashcards**, and glue or tape.

How to play ➡

1 Split the words into individual graphemes. Write each grapheme onto flashcards.

2 Take the vowel graphemes and stick them around the middle of one of the tins, so that if you twist the tin, a different one comes to the front.

3 In the same way, stick three or four of the other graphemes to each of the other tins.

4 Line up the tins, placing the one with vowel graphemes near the middle of the row.

5 Twist them so that one grapheme is showing at the front of each tin.

6 Ask your child to twist and move the tins until they can build a word using some or all of the tins.

Make it easier...

✹ You build one or two words first and then ask your child to have a go.

Make it harder...

✹ Can your child find a word that has one or more **consonant clusters**?

Add a twist
How many words can your child build in one minute?

PEACH
SLICES

TOP TIP:
When your child becomes more confident in reading and spelling, play this game with more cans so they can build longer words.

SENTENCE SPIES

What's the game?

In this game, your child reads and writes whole sentences containing words with the same letter pattern. Using words in a real sentence helps your child to remember them.

You will need

➡ Blank **flashcards** – some long and some short – and a pen or pencil.

➡ A group of words with a common **grapheme** that your child is ready to practise. If you'd like some help choosing which graphemes to focus on, go to the Worst Lists on pages 88-93.

Before you play

★ Make up a sentence using as many of the words from your group of words as possible. Write it down. Write it again without those key words and write the key words on separate flashcards, e.g.

I had to wait in the rain for the train

I had to ___ in the ___ for the ___

train

rain

wait

How to play ⇒

1 Read the full sentence with your child. Can they spot the words with the same pattern?

2 Now read the incomplete sentence. Can your child choose the correct words to put into the right gaps?

3 Finally, have a look at the key words together: identify the separate graphemes and the sounds that they represent. If you take the individual word cards away, can your child write the missing words into the gaps?

Make it harder...

* Think of another word that has the same common grapheme. Can your child work out how it is spelt?

* Can your child make up another sentence that uses these and other words with the same common grapheme? Can they try to write it?

77

CUT AND SWAP

What's the game?

In this game, your child cuts up written words to build new words, developing key reading and spelling skills.

You will need

➡ Blank **flashcards**, children's scissors and a pen or pencil.

➡ A group of words with a common **grapheme** for your child to practise. If your common grapheme was 'o', for example, you might use 'hot', 'pot', 'dot', etc.

How to play ➡ ➡ ➡ ➡ ➡

1 Write one of the words onto a flashcard , e.g. 'pot'. Split the other words into graphemes and write each grapheme onto a flashcard, leaving out the common grapheme that is already in your first word.

2 Ask your child to cut the whole word (pot) into graphemes. Can your child recall the sounds that each grapheme makes and then blend those sounds into a whole word to read out?

3 Point out the common grapheme that is in all of the words (in this case **o**).

4 Ask your child to use the common grapheme and some other graphemes to build a new word. How many new words can your child find?

Make it harder...

✱ Take away one or two of the graphemes. Remind your child of one of the words that they have already built that used one of the now-missing graphemes. Can your child remember the missing grapheme, write it onto a blank flashcard and build the word?

Make it harder STILL...

✱ Think of a new word with the same common grapheme, which includes a grapheme that you haven't used yet in the game. Can your child recall the grapheme needed, write it onto a blank flashcard and build the word?

SENTENCE BUILDER

What's the game?

In this game, your child writes whole sentences containing words with the same pattern. Remembering how to write a range of words that have the same pattern, and writing them in a sentence, builds key spelling skills and develops spelling knowledge.

You will need

➡ Paper and a pen or pencil.

➡ A group of words with a common **grapheme** that your child is ready to practise. If you'd like some help choosing which graphemes to focus on, go to the Word Lists on pages 88-93.

How to play ➡➡➡➡➡➡➡➡➡➡➡➡➡➡➡➡➡➡➡➡➡

1. Make up a sentence using as many of the words from your group of words as possible.

2. Tell your child the key sound that lots of words in your sentence share. Together, discuss and write down the grapheme that represents that sound.

3. Now tell your child the sentence that you have made up – for example: 'Shout it out loud – "I'm proud!"'

4. Ask your child to use the grapheme that you have already written to help them write the whole sentence.

Make it easier...

✳ You write one of the key words first, before asking your child to write the whole sentence.

Further games for tricky or difficult words

FEEL AND READ

What's the game?

In this hands-on craft game, your child feels the shapes of all the letters and letter groups in a word to help them remember how to read and write the word.

You will need

➡ A word or group of words with a common **grapheme** that your child is ready to practise.

➡ A few pieces of paper, a glue stick and glitter or sand.

How to play ➡

1 With your child, use glue to write a word from your group of words onto a piece of paper in large, neat letters. Cover the glue with glitter or something similar.

2 Repeat with a few other words from the set.

3 When dry, choose one of the words and sound it out with your child as they feel it with their finger. Can they blend together the different sounds to read the word?

4 Do the same with the other words.

5 Now can your child look at the words and read them without touching them?

TOP TIP:
If you don't have any glitter or sand, you could stick sequins, wool or tissue paper balls onto the glue to create the textured letters.

Make it harder...

✸ Can your child cut the words into graphemes, muddle them up and then sort them out again?

✸ Ask your child to copy the words, with a pen, onto separate pieces of paper. Can they now read their copies of the words?

✸ After you have looked at one of the words closely together, can your child write it from memory?

LOVELY LARGE WORDS

What's the game?

In this physical game, writing big, bold words helps your child to remember spellings.

You will need

➡ A word or group of words with a common **grapheme** that your child is ready to practise. If you'd like some help choosing which graphemes to focus on, go to the Word Lists on pages 88-93.

➡ A tool to draw huge letters, e.g. a mop, chalk or marker pen.

➡ Something to draw on.

How to play ➡

1 Write down one of your words in huge letters.

2 Ask your child to trace over your written word, saying each of the sounds as they trace the graphemes.

3 Now see whether your child can write the word independently, again saying the sounds as they write the graphemes.

4 Can your child now write the word with smaller letters on a piece of paper?

5 Repeat with other words if you are using a set of words.

Add a twist

Write the word with joined-up handwriting, which can help children to remember.

TOP TIP:

If your child struggles with step 3 (writing the words independently), try writing the words first as a dot-to-dot to give them a guide.

FEEL AND WRITE

What's the game?

In this game, sand or flour highlights the feeling of writing a word. This helps your child to remember how to spell it.

You will need

➡ A word or group of words with a common **grapheme** that your child is ready to practise. If you'd like some help choosing which graphemes to focus on, go to the Word Lists on pages 88-93.

➡ **Flashcards**, a tray and some sand, flour or something similar.

How to play ➡

1 Write your word, or words, onto flashcards.

2 Pour a little sand, or something similar, into the tray.

3 Show your child one of the words. Read it together, highlighting each grapheme and the sound it represents. Read it again, asking your child to trace over the letters with their finger.

4 Ask your child to write the word in the sand with their finger, whilst still looking at the written word. Ask them to say the sounds in the word as they write the letters.

5 Can your child write the word in the sand again, but this time without looking at the written word?

6 Now can your child write the word on a large, blank flashcard?

7 If you have chosen a group of words, do the same with the other words, noticing the parts of all the words that are the same.

Add a twist

Write the words onto flashcards with joined-up handwriting. Ask your child to trace the joined-up words and then to try to copy them joined-up into the sand.

WORDPLAY

What's the game?

This is a collection of little word games that your child can choose from to help memorise spellings.

How to play ➡➡➡➡➡➡➡➡➡➡➡➡➡➡➡➡➡➡➡➡➡➡➡➡

1. Look at the word, or word group, with your child. Discuss things you could do to the words to make them easier to remember. These could include:

   a splitting them into separate graphemes: c ou l d

   b highlighting the common pattern:
   c ou l d, sh ou l d, w ou l d

   c highlighting any difficult bits in the words: c ou l d

   d making a silly sentence out of some or all of the letters in the word: c **ould**: o u lucky duck!

   e making a silly sentence out of the group of words with the same pattern: Should I eat it? I would if I could!

   f drawing or finding a picture that reminds you of the words, or of one of your silly sentences

   g writing the word in a special way – for example, with big letters, joined-up writing, in sand or with clay.

2. Practise tracing, reading and writing the word, or words, with the help of your new approaches, and then practise again without them.

TOP TIP:
Games and activities for tricky words are covered in more detail on pages 80-93.

GET THE MEANING, FILL THE GAP

What's the game?

In this game, your child learns that remembering the meaning of a word part can help them to read and spell the word.

You will need

➡ A common additional **word part** that your child is ready to practise reading or spelling and a few words that your word part can be added to. For a list of common additional word parts, and words that use them, see the list of suffixes on page 94.

➡ Some flashcards, paper and pens or pencils.

Before you play

★ Write each word onto a flashcard. Then write them again onto fresh flashcards, but with the ending added. For example, 'like' and 'liked' and 'stop' and 'stopped'. Remember to make changes to the original spelling if needed.

How to play ➡

1 Read the words with your child, discussing their meaning and noticing any changes when the ending is added.

2 Make up a silly sentence that needs one of the words, either with or without the ending. For example, 'I really like ice cream'.

3 Say the sentence, but when you get to the chosen word, just say 'beeeep'. For example, 'I really beeeep ice cream'.

4 Ask your child to hold up the flashcard that will correctly fill the gap in the sentence. In this case, 'like'.

5 Try again with a few different sentences, some needing the ending and some not.

Make it harder...

✹ Look through the words again, paying special attention to any spelling changes.

✹ Say a sentence again and ask your child to fill the gap, but this time by writing the correct word onto a blank flashcard.

LOOK, SAY, TRACE, COVER, WRITE

What's the game?

This popular game uses memory and repetition, along with a range of other strategies, to help your child remember spellings.

Catch the cat! He's out of the kitchen and into the hutch to fetch the rabbit for tea!

Word	Tip	Write and trace	Try 1	Try 2
kitchen	ki **tch** en	kitchen	kitchen	kitchen
catch	ca **tch**			
hutch	hu **tch**			
fetch	fe **tch**			

You will need

➡ A word or group of words with a common letter pattern – **grapheme** – that your child is ready to practise. If you'd like some help choosing which graphemes to focus on, go to the Word Lists on pages 88-93.

➡ Paper, an eraser and a pen or pencil.

How to play ➡

1 Draw a simple table on your piece of paper, with a few columns and rows.

2 Write the words from your word list in the first column.

3 Look at the words listed with your child. Discuss things you could do to the words to make them easier to remember.

4 In the second column, write the words again, but this time include the helpful approaches you have thought of.

5 If you're using a group of words with a common pattern, try to make up a silly sentence using as many of the words as possible and write it on the piece of paper too.

6 Ask your child to trace the first word, whilst looking at it and saying the sounds represented by each grapheme. Now cover the word and see whether your child can write it neatly with a pencil in the next column.

7 If your child gets the first word right, move on to the next word. If not, rub out the attempt and try again.

8 Keep going until all of the words have been practised. Do this a few times over a week.

Sound List

Below is a list of the 44 single sounds, or **phonemes**, that we use in English.

/b/ – bat	/s/ – sun	/a/ – ant	/oi/ – coin
/k/ – cat	/t/ – tap	/e/ – egg	/ar/ – farm
/d/ – dog	/v/ – van	/i/ – in	/or/ – for
/f/ – fan	/w/ – wig	/o/ – on	/ur/ – hurt
/g/ – go	/y/ – yes	/u/ – up	/air/ – fair
/h/ – hen	/z/ – zip	/ai/ – rain	/ear/ – dear
/j/ – jet	/sh/ – shop	/ee/ – feet	/ure/ – sure
/l/ – leg	/ch/ – chip	/igh/ – night	/ə/ – corner (the 'schwa' is an unstressed vocal sound which is close to /u/)
/m/ – map	/th/ – thin	/oa/ – boat	
/n/ – net	**/th/** – then	**/oo/** – boot	
/p/ – pen	/ng/ – ring	/oo/ – look	
/r/ – rat	/zh/ – vision	/ow/ – cow	

This phoneme table lists the 44 phonemes of the English language, taken from the National Strategies Standards' phonics sounds (DfES, 2007).

Word Lists

The table on the following pages shows the phases in which different **graphemes** - letters or groups of letters that represent one sound - are generally introduced to children. The grapheme list and accompanying word lists are based on 'Letters and sounds: Principles and practice of high-quality phonics', the UK government's phonics teaching programme published in 2007.

Common **CVC words** taught in phases 2 and 3 are given in **bold**.

* *indicates dependent on accent (see 'a' making 'ar' sound)*

Word Lists

Phase 1

In first phase of teaching letters and sounds, children learn to hear individual sounds on their own and in words – see pages 29-39 (games).

Phase 2

Grapheme	Sample word lists
s	**sat, sap, sit, Sam, gas**
a	an, at, **Sam, sat**
t	at, **sat, tin, top, tap**
p	**pat, sap, pot**
i	**pin, bit, pip, sip**, it, is
n	**pin**, an, in, **nip, tin, nap, tan**
m	**mat, man, map, Sam**, am, **mam**
d	**dad, sad, did, Sid, dip, din**
g	**got, gap, tag, pig, gas**
o	**top, not, got, dog, God, pot**
c	**cat, cup, cot, cop, cod**
k	**kit, kid, Kim, Ken**
ck	**sock, sack, kick**
e	**get, pet, ten**
u	up, **mum, run, mug, sun, tuck**
r	**rim, rip, rat, rug**, rocket
h	**had, him, his, hut, hop, hug, has, hat**
b	**big, but, bad, Ben, bat, bed, bug, bag, bus**
f	if, of, **fit, fig, fun, fog**
ff	**puff, cuff, huff, off**
l	**lap, lot, let, leg, lit**
ll	**doll, Nell, dull, Bill, fill, bell, tell, sell**
ss	**less, hiss, pass, kiss, Tess, fuss, mess**

Word Lists

Phase 3

Grapheme	Sample word lists
j	**jam**, **Jill**, **jet**, **jog**, **Jack**,
v	**van**, **vet**, **Vic**, Kevin, **visit**
w	**win**, **wag**, **web**, **wax**, wicked
x	**mix**, **fix**, **box**, **tax**, **six**, taxi, exit
y	**yes**, **yet**, **yell**, **yap**, yum-yum
z	**zip**, **Zak**, zigzag
zz	**buzz**, **jazz**
qu	**quiz**, **quick**, **quit**, **quick**, **quack**
ch	**chop**, **chin**, **chug**, **check**, **such**, **chip**, **chill**, **much**, **rich**, chicken
sh	**ship**, **shop**, **shed**, **shell**, **fish**, **shock**, **cash**, **bash**, **hush**
th	**them**, **then**, **that**, **this**, **with**
th	**moth**, **thin**, **thick**, **path**, **bath**
ng	**ring**, **rang**, **hang**, **song**, **wing**, **rung**, **king**, **long**, **sing**
ai	**rain**, **train**, **wait**, **fail**
ee	**see**, **feel**, **weep**, **feet**, **jeep**, **week**, **meet**, **deep**, **keep**
igh	high, **light**, sigh, **night**, **might**, **fight**, **tight**, tonight
oa	**coat**, **soap**, **road**, **goat**, **load**, oak, **toad**, **boat**
oo	too, zoo, **boot**, **hoof**, **zoom**, **cool**, **food**, **root**, **moon**, **roof**
oo	**look**, **foot**, **cook**, **good**, **book**, **took**, **wood**, **wool**, **hook**, **hood**
ar	far, **farm**, bar, **dart**, **cart**, **card**, **hard**, **jar**, **lard**, **Mark**, **part**, **tart**, **yard**
or	for, **fork**, **cork**, **sort**, **born**, **torn**, **fort**
ur	fur, **burn**, **burp**, **curl**, **hurt**, turn, turnip
ow	now, **down**, cow, how, bow, row, **town**
oi	oil, **boil**, **coin**, **coil**, **join**, **soil**, **toil**, poison, **foil**
ear	ear, **fear**, **rear**, clear
air	air, **fair**, **chair**
ure	sure, pure, cure, secure, mature, manure
er	boxer, teacher, speaker, singer, longer

Phase 4

During phase 4, children learn to read and spell longer words and words with consonant clusters.

Grapheme	Sample word lists
st	stop, step, nest
nd	end, hand, bend
mp	lamp, bump, camp
nt	bent, rent, pant, tent
nk	ink, honk, link
ft	gift, lift, raft
sk	skull, skin, skirt
lt	belt, melt, kilt
lp	help, gulp
lf	wolf, calf, half
lk	milk, walk, talk
pt	kept, slept, leapt
xt	text
tr	train, tree, try
dr	draw, dry, drink
gr	green, grass, grey
cr	cry, crisp, crown
br	brush, brown, brick
fr	frog, frost, fridge
bl	black, block, blow
fl	flag, fly, flap
gl	glass, glow, glide
pl	play, plum, plate
cl	clown, cloud, clap
sl	slip, slide, slug
sp	spoon, sponge, spam
st	stop, stick, stack
tw	twig, twins
sm	smoke, smile
pr	pram, prize, press
sc	scarf, escape
sk	skirt, skunk
sn	snow, snail
nch	bench, bunch, crunch
scr	screen, screech, screw
shr	shrub, shrug
thr	three, throw, thrust
str	string, strong, strip

Word Lists

Phase 5

Grapheme	Sample word lists
ay	day, ray, say, may, lay, slay
ou	out, sound, about, pound, ounce, loud
ie	tie, pie, lie, die
ea	eat, bean, mean, meat, lean, reap, leap, leak, reach, speak
oy	boy, toy, Roy
ir	girl, dirt, shirt, fir, skirt
ue	blue, Sue
aw	saw, dawn, yawn, law
wh	when, what, which, why
ph	photo
ew	new, stew
oe	toe, doe, foe, hoe, Joe
au	Paul
a-e (ai)	make, snake, made, came, late, amaze
e-e (ee)	these
i-e (ie)	like
o-e (oa)	home, woke, note, those, bone, phone
u-e (ue)	cube
s	treasure, measure, leisure
i	find, mind, sign
o	cold, fold, bold, bolt
c (s)	cent, receive
g	giant, generous
u	put
ow	blow, sow, flown, slow, show
ie	field, fierce, pierce, relief
ea	bread, thread, dread, health, spread
er	her, fern, serve, term, nerve
a	what, wash, swap, swallow
y	by, sky, fry, my, shy, sty, why
y	very, berry, sadly, happy
ch	school, chemist, echo, chorus
ch	chef, machine, chute, parachute
ou	shoulder, boulder
ou	you, group, youth, coupon
ou	four, course, court
ou	double, cousin, country
oul	could, would, should

Word Lists

Grapheme	Sample word lists
t (ch)	picture, adventure, furniture, mixture, future
tch (ch)	catch, fetch, pitch, notch, crutch, stitch
dge (j)	fudge, hedge, bridge, badge, badger
mb (m)	lamb, comb, thumb, climb, plumber, crumb
gn (n)	gnat, gnome, sign, design, gnash
kn (n)	knit, knob, knot, knee, knock, knife, know, knew, knight
wr (r)	wrap, wren, wrong, wrench, write, wrote, wreck, wry, written
st (s)	listen, whistle, bristle, glisten, rustle, jostle, castle, bustle, Christmas
se (s)	house, mouse, grease, crease, horse, gorse, purse, loose
se (z)	please, tease, ease, browse, cheese, noise, pause, blouse, because
o (u)	some, come, done, none, son, nothing, month, mother, brother
y (i)	gym, crystal, mystery, sympathy, pyramid
ey (ee)	donkey, valley, monkey, trolley, pulley, chimney, Lesley
ere (ear)	here, severe, interfere, adhere
eer (ear)	beer, deer, jeer, cheer, peer, seer, sheer, veer, career
a (ar*)	bath, path, father, last, grass, afternoon, pass
al (ar)	calm, palm, balm, half, calf
ere (air)	there, where, nowhere, somewhere, everywhere
ear (air)	pear, bear, wear, tear, swear
are (air)	bare, care, dare, fare, mare, square, scare, share, stare
al (or)	talk, walk, stalk, chalk
a (or)	all, call, fall, ball
our (or)	four, pour, your, court, fourth, tour, mourn, fourteen
augh (or)	caught, taught, naughty, daughter
ear (ur)	learn, earn, earth, pearl, early, search, heard, earnest, rehearsal
or (ur)	word, work, world, worm, worth, worse, worship, worst
u (oo*)	put, push, pull, full, bush, bull, cushion, pudding, playful
ay (ai)	day, play, may, say, stray, clay, spray, tray, crayon, delay
ow (oa)	low, grow, snow, glow, tow, show, slow, window, row
oe (oa)	toe, foe, Joe, goes
ue (y-oo)	cue, due, hue, venue, value, pursue, queue, statue, argue

* indicates dependent on accent (see 'a' making 'ar' sound)

List of Suffixes

Below is a list of word parts often added to the ends of words to change the meaning of those words. These word parts are known as **suffixes**.

Words in **bold** are words in which the original word has to change when certain endings are added. The change to the original word will either be changing a letter, missing a letter or doubling a letter.

When looking at these endings with children, help them to notice any changes in meaning and in spelling that they cause to the original word.

Word part / suffix	Sample word list
s	cats, parks, dogs, boys, girls, toys
s	runs, barks, walks, jumps, thinks
es	bunches, bushes, boxes, **puppies, bunnies**
es	pushes, washes, buzzes, **marries, flies**
ed	walked, jumped, picked, **baked, hurried, skipped**
ing	playing, walking, staying, **using, putting**
ful	playful, wonderful, careful
est	slowest, greatest, **biggest, happiest, latest**
ly	slowly, badly, **happily, rudely**
ness	darkness, sadness, **happiness, silliness**
y	sandy, **funny, smoky**

Glossary

Useful words and phrases:

blend	To join sounds together to build whole spoken words: 'C' – 'a' – 't' = 'cat'.
consonant cluster	Consonants next to each other in a word that keep their separate sounds, e.g. 'p' and 'l' in 'play'.
consonant sounds	Closed sounds, i.e. sounds that we make by blocking air with our lips, teeth or tongue. All sounds that are not vowels are called consonants. Consonants sounds are represented by all of the letters in the alphabet apart from a, e, i, o, u and y, either on their own or in groups. Examples are: t, b, sh, th, ff.
CVC word	Word with three sounds – a consonant, then a vowel, then a consonant, e.g. cat (c – a – t), ship (sh – i – p).
flashcard	Paper or card cut into small rectangles, big enough to write some letters or words on.
grapheme	A letter, or group of letters, that represents one sound, e.g. sh, t, ck.
phoneme	A single sound.
phoneme–grapheme correspondence	The relationship between a sound and the letter or letters that represent that sound. Words have the same 'phoneme–grapheme correspondence' if they have some matching sounds represented by the same letters, e.g. w**ai**t, r**ai**n, tr**ai**n.
phonics	Teaching and learning the relationship between individual sounds and the letters that represent them.
segment	To split a spoken word into individual sounds.
syllable	A beat in a word. Each beat, or syllable, has one vowel sound, e.g. **do** has one beat/syllable; **un do** has two beats/syllables; **un do ing** has three beats/syllables.
vowel sounds	'Open' sounds, i.e. the sounds that we make without blocking air with our lips, teeth or tongue. All sounds that are not consonants are vowels. Vowel sounds are represented by the letters a, e, i, o, u, sometimes y and by combinations of these and other letters. Examples are: a, e, i, o, u, y, ai, ee, ou, oo, ee, a-e, igh, eigh, aigh.

References

Department for Education and Skills (DfES) (2007), 'Letters and sounds: principles and practice of high-quality phonics'. Available at: **https://www.gov.uk/government/publications/letters-and-sounds** (accessed 21/11/18).

Rose, J. (2006), **Independent Review of the Teaching of Early Reading.** Department for Education and Skills.

Further reading

Bosman, A. M. T. and Van Orden, G. C. (1997), 'Why spelling is more difficult than reading', in C. A. Perfetti, L. Rieben and M. Fayol (eds), **Learning to Spell: Research, Theory, and Practice Across Languages.** Mahwah, NJ, US: Lawrence Erlbaum Associates Publishers, pp. 173–194.

Department for Children, Schools and Families (2008), 'The impact of parental involvement on children's education'. Available at: **https://webarchive.nationalarchives.gov.uk/20120504214534/https://www.education.gov.uk/publications/eOrderingDownload/DCSF-Parental_Involvement.pdf** (accessed 26/11/18).

Department for Education (2013), 'English programmes of study: key stages 1 and 2: national curriculum in England'. Available at: **https://assets.publishing.service.gov.uk/government/uploads/system/uploads/attachment_data/file/335186/PRIMARY_national_curriculum_-_English_220714.pdf** (accessed 26/11/18).

Ehri, L., Nunes, S., Stahl, S. and Willows, D. (2001), 'Systematic phonics instruction helps students learn to read: evidence from National Reading Panel's meta-analysis'. **Review of Educational Research**, 71, (3), 393–447.

Fisher, B., Cozens, M. E. and Greive, C. (2007), 'Look-say-cover-write-say-check and old way/new way – mediational learning: a comparison of the effectiveness of two tutoring programs for children with persistent spelling difficulties', **Special Education Perspectives**, 16, (1), 19–38.

Joliffe, W., Waugh, D. and Carss, A. (2012), **Teaching Systematic Synthetic Phonics in Primary Schools.** London: Sage Publications Ltd.

Kelly, K. and Phillips, S. (2011), **Teaching Literacy to Learners with Dyslexia: A Multi-Sensory Approach.** London: Sage.

Mann, T. B., Bushell, D. and Morris, E. K. (2010), 'Use of sounding out to improve spelling in young children'. **Journal of Applied Behaviour Analysis**, 43, (1), 89–93.

Miller, L. J., Rakes, T. A. and Choate, J. S. (1997), 'Handwriting and spelling: tools for communication', in J. S. Choate (ed), **Successful Inclusive Teaching** (4th edition). Boston: Allyn and Bacon, pp.214–247.

Montgomery, D. (2012), 'The contribution of handwriting and spelling remediation to overcoming dyslexia', in T. Wydell and L. Fern-Pollack (eds), **Dyslexia: A Comprehensive and International Approach.** Croatia: IntechOpen, pp. 109–146. Available at: **https://www.intechopen.com/books/dyslexia-a-comprehensive-and-international-approach** (accessed 26/11/18).

Nunes, T., Bryant, P. and Barros, R. (2012), 'The development of word recognition and its significance for comprehension and fluency', **Journal of Educational Psychology**, 104, (4), 959–973.

Phillips, W. E. and Feng, J. (2012), 'Methods for sight word recognition in kindergarten: traditional flashcard method vs. multisensory approach'. Paper presented at the 2012 Annual Conference of Georgia Educational Research Association, October 18–20, 2012. Savannah, Georgia. Available at: **http://files.eric.ed.gov/fulltext/ED536732.pdf** (accessed 5/5/2015).

Robinson, K. (2016), **A Creative Approach to Teaching Phonics.** London: Bloomsbury Education.

Shams L. and Seitz, A. (2008), 'Benefits of multisensory learning', **Trends in Cognitive Sciences**, 12, (11), 411–417.

Shoval, E. (2011), 'Using mindful movement in cooperative learning while learning about angles'. **Instructional Science**, 39, (4), 453–466.

Waugh, D., Warner, C. and Waugh, R. (2013), **Teaching Grammar, Punctuation and Spelling in Primary Schools.** London: Sage Publications Ltd.

Westwood, P. (2014) **Teaching Spelling: Exploring Common Sense Strategies and Best Practices.** Oxon: Routledge.